S0-ARV-711

ideals® EASTER

More Than 50 Years of Celebrating Life's Most Treasured Moments

Vol. 56, No. 1

"Oh, world as God has made it! All is beauty."
—*Robert Browning*

IDEALS—Vol. 56, No. 1 January MCMXCIX IDEALS (ISSN 0019-137X) is published six times a year: January, March, May, July, September, and November by IDEALS PUBLICATIONS INCORPORATED, 535 Metroplex Drive, Suite 250, Nashville, TN 37211. Periodical postage paid at Nashville, Tennessee, and additional mailing offices.
Copyright © MCMXCIX by IDEALS PUBLICATIONS INCORPORATED.
POSTMASTER: Send address changes to Ideals, PO Box 305300, Nashville, TN 37230. All rights reserved.
Title IDEALS registered U.S. Patent Office.

SINGLE ISSUE—U.S. $5.95 USD; Higher in Canada; ONE-YEAR SUBSCRIPTION—U.S. $19.95 USD; Canada $36.00 CDN (incl. GST and shipping); Foreign $25.95 USD; TWO-YEAR SUBSCRIPTION—U.S. $35.95 USD; Canada $66.50 CDN (incl. GST and shipping); Foreign $47.95 USD

The cover and entire contents of IDEALS are fully protected by copyright and must not be reproduced in any manner whatsoever. Printed and bound in USA by Quebecor Printing. Printed on Weyerhaeuser Husky.

The paper used in this publication meets the minimum requirements of American National Standard for Information Sciences—Permanence of Paper for Printed Library Materials, ANSI Z39.48-1984.

Subscribers may call customer service at 1-800-558-4343 to make address changes.
Unsolicited manuscripts will not be returned without a self-addressed, stamped envelope.

ISBN 0-8249-1153-9 GST 131903775

Cover Photo
SPRINGTIME BOUQUET
Photograph by
Nancy Matthews

Inside Front Cover
VASE DE FLEURS
Marie Laurencin, artist
Christie's Images

Inside Back Cover
VASE DE FLEURS
J. Selmersheim-Desgrange, artist
Christie's Images

It Is pring Again

Zelda PenDell Leonard

Petals falling softly
Like snow upon the ground;
Dappled sunshine spreading
Its glory all around;
Fleecy clouds asailing
Across the sky of blue,
Blown by breezes gentle—
Spring is here anew.
Brooks that murmur gently
Over beds of stone;
Bird-notes sweetly calling
Songs of lilting tone;
Violets shyly hiding
Underneath the trees
While above comes softly
The buzzing of the bees.
Earth fulfills its promise;
Joys it e'er will bring.
Our hearts rejoice to welcome
The blessedness of spring.

A ream

Percy Bysshe Shelley

I dreamed that, as I wandered by the way,
Bare winter suddenly was changed to spring,
And gentle odours led my steps astray,
Mixed with a sound of waters murmuring
Along a shelving bank of turf, which lay
Under a copse, and hardly dared to fling
Its green arms round the bosom of the stream,
But kissed it and then fled, as thou mightest in a dream.

A rock garden explodes with spring color in Baileys Harbor, Wisconsin. Photograph by Darryl Beers.

Rebirth

Ruth K. Stroh

I watched the dawn's all golden glow
Reach down upon the sand.
It was as if our God Himself
Had taken earth's dear hand.

Earth met the sky in gentleness,
Dispelling nightly gloom.
A tender stroke, a bit of love,
Stretched over nature's room.

The world was pink and blue and gold;
Our earth was kissed with dew,
Paletted by the master brush—
A universe anew!

A spectacular pink sunrise complements a field of yellow canola near
Colfax, Washington. Photograph by Dennis Frates/Oregon Scenics.

The Florist's
Window

Martha D. Tourison

The sprays of pussy willows on display,
Created by the florist's skillful hands,
Embedded in a vase with lilac strands
And violets and jonquils in array;
The purple and the yellow and the gray,
In medley of all colors spring expands,
Despite wild March's blust'ry reprimands
That we not rush the season in this way.
I'll lightly trip in slippers that are red.
My frock will be a gay beribboned thing.
I'll come again to watch the florist trim
His window, and I'm sure he'll turn his head
As there I stand in colors that will bring
The hope he gave to me right back to him.

Overleaf: Each spring, this orchard in Yamhill County, Oregon, offers seemingly endless lines of cherry trees draped in white blossoms. Photograph by Steve Terrill.
Opposite: An array of colorful blooms beckons visitors to this florist's shop. Photograph by H. Armstrong Roberts.

HANDMADE HEIRLOOM

A handmade clay vase is the perfect home for a spray of silk rhododendron.

CLAY VASE
Nancy Skarmeas

Up until a few years ago, my grandmother always had beautiful gardens surrounding her home. Gramma spent long hours fussing over her flowers—weeding, watering, and just admiring—and they blossomed perfectly from the first days of spring well into the cool of fall. But with the death of my aunt, who had been Gramma's constant companion since the death of my grandfather, Gramma became lonely. Soon the upkeep on the house became too much for her, and she moved in with another daughter. My aunt suggested she transplant some of her own flowers to the new yard, but Gramma rejected the idea. Although she missed her gardens, she didn't feel up to starting new ones.

We all tried to cheer Gramma with bouquets of fresh flowers. She thanked us and said they were beautiful, but she didn't seem as pleased as we hoped. And then one day a friend of hers brought over a dozen beautiful red roses—silk roses. Gramma loved them. These artificial flowers—something we would never have thought to buy for her—truly made her happy. The fresh flower arrangements we had given her faded within days, but these roses were continuously lovely.

I thought about Gramma and those flowers when I came upon a kit for making a pottery vase at home using the kitchen oven. I had always wanted to try pottery but had been put off by the need to find a kiln to fire the piece. Now here was a project that I could do without a kiln—and although the instructions warned that the vase would be unable to hold water, I wasn't concerned. In fact, I was pleased. My pottery vase would not need to hold water because it would hold silk flowers for Gramma.

When I began to look into making my own clay pottery piece, I discovered that I would be following an ancient tradition of creating art from the earth itself. Claywork is one of the oldest of art forms and is represented in sculpture from the early Chinese dynasties and in the tiles of Persian mosques. Working with clay can be challenging, and many artists use a potter's wheel, glazes, and kilns. The age-old handbuilding techniques, however, require no special tools. Most craft stores today offer oven-baked clay, which is a favorite not only with grade-school art teachers but also with any artists or crafters eager to try their hand at this ancient art.

The package of oven-baked clay I purchased came in several colors, including brown and terra cotta, and even listed a phone number I could call if I had technical questions. Also included were basic directions for working with clay. After browsing through some library books on pottery making for inspiration, I decided on the basic shape of my vase and chose to use a method called the coiling technique to create it.

First, I rolled a portion of clay into a round ball and flattened the ball to form a circular base. I then rolled a clump of clay into a coil the length of the circumference of the vase. After attaching the coil to the base, I repeated the process with several more coils until the vase was the desired height. I lightly smoothed the joints on the exterior of my vase, but you may choose to leave the coiled appearance. You can also use household items to add texture to the surface. Once you complete the construction of your project, you must let it dry thoroughly before baking it in your kitchen oven according to the package directions.

What I enjoyed most about working with clay is this: not only was I able to design the shape of my project, I was able to decorate it as well. Before painting my vase, I sealed it by brushing on a solution of diluted white craft glue and allowing it to dry. Then, using latex craft paints, I was able to bring the beauty of Gramma's garden to my project with a floral design in bright spring colors.

I am going to bring my handmade clay vase to Gramma on Easter Sunday. Flowers on Easter are a tradition for us, and this year will be no different. But in my vase this year will be Easter lilies made of the finest white silk. We have all tried so hard to make Gramma happy in her new home, to make it just like the home she enjoyed for the past fifty years. Although she may no longer be able to enjoy the blooms in her outdoor garden, she is sure to smile every time she walks by my Easter gift, for the silk lilies and the colorful clay vase will always bloom as brightly as the gardens of her memories.

Nancy Skarmeas is a book editor and mother of a three-year-old son, Gordon, who keeps her and her husband quite busy at their home in New Hampshire.

Creation

I never see a butterfly
Or hear a singing bird,
But what in some strange manner I
Am very deeply stirred.

Who first conceived the tender wings
On which it seeks the rose?
Has human thought such lovely things
To fashion and disclose?

O singing bird upon a tree!
Has ever human mind
Contrived to solve the mystery
Of how you were designed?

Man writes his loftiest thoughts in words
And builds with brick and stone.
But dreams of butterflies and birds
Belong to God alone.

Edgar A. Guest began his illustrious career in 1895 at the age of fourteen, when his work first appeared in the Detroit Free Press. His column was syndicated in over three hundred newspapers, and he became known as "The Poet of the People."

Patrick McRae has created art for Ideals for more than a decade. A Wisconsin native, he was educated at the Milwaukee Institute of Art and Design and lives with his wife and three children. He enjoys coaching his children's soccer and baseball teams.

A Song of Spring

Nora M. Bozeman

April sings a song of spring
And dances on a bluebird's wing.
Tulips raise their heads to view
A cloud-draped sky of azure hue.

Shiny dewdrops dress the days
In gowns of silver-sparkled rays.
Breezes rustle newborn leaves
And wrap them in wind symphonies.

Sometimes sunshine, sometimes showers
Bathe and nurture budding flowers
As April sings a song of spring
And dances on a bluebird's wing.

A male eastern bluebird perches proudly among the columbine blooms. Photograph by Gay Bumgarner.

A rose provides a resting spot for this male eastern bluebird. Photograph by Gay Bumgarner.

The Transient

Betty Cornwell

A bluebird paused beneath my eave
Upon his transitory flight.
With not so much as "by your leave,"
He settled sweetly for the night.

But peeping from my windowsill
Across the misty morning yard,
I only found one azure quill—
A most celestial calling card!

The Waking Earth

As I look upon the green of hills, I can sense the rebirth of the earth. The hills turn young again, and spring endows the land with sun and song. I can almost hear the whisper of the land as it rouses from its winter of sleep. It is a resurrection, the birth and renewal of life. Nature feels it, and so do I.

The birds sing of this welcome rebirth. Within my own dooryard I listen to the robin and bluebird, the morning dove and cardinal, the chickadee, titmouse, and mocker. I hear the song in the piping chorus of the peepers in the bogs not far away and in the ok-a-lee of the redwing in the marsh. I see it too in the changing color of the goldfinch at the feeder in the yard.

Buds and bulbs and blooms respond to the warming fingers and soft spring showers of the vernal season. The hyacinth, crocus, and daffodil bring beauty to once-sleeping flower beds. Violets spring into bloom while dandelions push up their golden bonnets in the dooryard grass. Thrift spreads its mounds of pink along the roadbank, and the orchard on the far hill takes on the soft pink glow of the peach trees.

I too feel the touch of spring. I await the chance to return to the land, to feel the well-worn handles of the plow in my hands. I want to watch the furrows being turned to the sun by the shining share of the plow. I want to listen to the creaking harness of the team. I want to be imbued with spring, to be a part once more of life's glorious rebirth and renewal.

The author of two published books, Lansing Christman has been contributing to Ideals for more than two decades. Mr. Christman has also been published in several American, foreign, and braille anthologies. He lives in rural South Carolina.

Clematis and rock cress interweave to form a colorful ground cover in Clackamas County, Oregon. Photograph by Steve Terrill.

Sowing Seeds

LaVerne P. Larson

Today I made a garden
In the rich and fertile sod,
And with every seed I planted
Felt a fellowship with God.

The sun looked down and smiled
While I spent each pleasant hour
Planning future beauty
Where Mother Earth would flower.

Breezes danced o'er fence and lawn
And kissed my cheek with glee;
Bright-eyed robins hopped around
And winked and chirped at me.

Fluffy clouds, like fleets of ships,
Sailed the sky-blue bowl;
A magic kind of happiness
Filled my heart and soul.

My mind was free to dream a while
And cast all cares away;
I stood at heaven's doorstep
When I sowed the seeds today.

A gardener displays her spring cuttings after a day among the flowers.
Photograph by Nancy Matthews.

In the Garden

Ilo Orleans

It's good to be back
At the soil again,
Out in the garden
To toil again.

It's good to plant
And to sow again,
To dig and to rake
And to hoe again.

I'm happy and merry:
I sing again,
Because today
It is Spring again.

A young girl enjoys a day of spring planting in artist Donald Zolan's painting Little Gardener, © Zolan Fine Arts, Hershey, Pennsylvania.

Remember When

FROM GOLDEN DAYS IN GRANDPA'S GARDEN
Marjorie Holmes

I grieve for the children who grow up missing gardens; the thrill of spying that first pinstripe of green that signals the seeds are up in spring. . . . When I was growing up, the garden was as much a part of the child's world as his mother's apron. Most of our food came straight from the garden. Also, the family garden was a kind of character symbol. The bigger and neater it was, the more worthy of respect. To have a little, scrabbly, half-hearted garden or a big unkempt one was to be labeled shiftless. And not to have a garden at all—well! . . .

It was impossible to hide the state of your garden. People walked more then and, strolling past, cast frankly appraising eyes. Also, your garden flowed right up to the alley which bisected every block. If you hadn't weeded clear back to that cindery avenue the iceman might notice, or Judge Bailey taking his shortcut home.

Gardeners, whatever their era or locale, are of the earth earthy. They garden out of love. Such was my Grandpa Griffith. His garden was his passion and his pride. Although his garden was smaller after Grandma died, it was always as neat as a Grant Wood painting, its products blue-ribbon winners at the county fair. To him it was vital that vegetables be sown on Good Friday, and potatoes be planted dark of the moon. "When the moon comes out they sprout," he solemnly averred. Although we tended to spurn this as superstition we did so at our

own risk. His potatoes *did* get to the table first, and always grew big and firm. Likewise, his radishes, green onions, and lettuce generally outdistanced all rivals. . . .

It was generally Grandpa who saved the family honor by lining up that prima donna of plowmen, Nate Mitchell, and his horse, Daisy, to plow up our backyard. . . . When the entire back lot had been transformed into a black and stormy sea, . . . the real business of gardening would begin.

Dad, balding young and chewing gum in his chipper way, would be both funny and tender as he adjudicated claims, guided wobbly hoes, and squatted to help eager fingers shake seeds into trenches and cover them carefully.

Then, after days of anxious watching, the miracle occurred. You rushed out one morning to discover a few beady trails of green. "The garden's up! Look, look." First, the round pushy radish leaves; then the tiny points of onions, and a delicate dance of lettuce sifting through. Astoundingly soon your mother was sending you out to see if any of this was big enough. And lo, probing among the radishes' prickly leaves, testing the spindly threads below, you uprooted a few rosy imp-faces with saucy tails. Among the delicate spears of the onions were a few pearly tips. And the lettuce was thick enough to cut, though the leaves were still so delicate and small they clung babylike to your fingers, especially when you washed them in a big dishpan under the pump.

Mother always greeted this virgin offering with childish elation. "Oh, I could make a *meal* out of fresh garden stuff!" she would cry, heaping the bowls and lavishing her own with vinegar, salt, and pepper. So could we all. For with a glass of milk and plenty of bread and butter, who could ask for more?

WRITE AT ONCE FOR YOUR COPY OF

Schling's
Garden Book

A beautiful Spring Catalog of the best in flowers and vegetables for your garden

...year it is more important than ever to get your request in early. The supply of catalogs ...necessarily limited. To be sure to get your copy, please write promptly.

DON'T MISS THIS WONDERFUL
VICTORY GARDEN SWEET CORN

A really sensational new variety of sweet...

The HOME
GARDE

...model... of sterilized starting medium...
supply of sterilized new seed starting medium, has...
successful new seed starting medium, has...
Complete kit, as illustrated, has...
boxes, 5½" long (each with 3 individual
seedling trays — 9 in all); bag of Mica-Gro; full
instructions; 2 pkts. of choice seeds (1 veg.,
1 flower)
Everything needed for an early start.............All for $1.00

Postpaid to Miss. River; West of Miss. River add 20¢.

COLLECTOR'S CORNER

ANTIQUE GARDENING TOOLS

by Maxine Johnson

I was not born a gardener but made one by life's unpredictable experiences. On the city block where I grew up, the closest thing to a garden was the little patch of grass between the sidewalk and the street. Flowers came from the neighborhood florist shop and vegetables came from the corner grocery. I married a boy from the neighborhood; we bought a house two blocks away from my parents' home and settled into city life. But then the unexpected happened. My husband was transferred, and we moved from urban Massachusetts to very rural Vermont. I had two small sons, no driver's license, and ten acres of land in the shadow of the Green Mountains.

Nature was everywhere, and nothing but nature. But still I was slow to warm to gardening. I started out with a few flowers in pots and eventually learned how to transplant them into the ground. Then the children and I decided to grow a couple of tomato plants, and soon we added peas, peppers, squash, and corn. When you live in the country, nature is your closest neighbor, and you either make friends or get lonely. So I made friends and began to mark the seasons with the flowers and the colors of the leaves. By the time the boys left for college, I was a first-rate gardener. Then something else unexpected happened. My husband retired early from his job, and we suddenly had time to explore our adopted home state. We started taking long drives, staying at country inns, and visiting antique shops; and that's where I discovered the world of antique gardening tools.

My collection of antique tools began with a small, weathered rake that I bought in an antique shop in a small New Hampshire town where my husband and I spent a glorious October weekend. The handle of the rake was once painted red, but time and the elements had faded the color. The shopkeeper told us that the diminutive rake was made sometime near the turn of the century for a child or for a lady, but I didn't much care about its age. I eyed it as the perfect size for my young nephew who visits often and shares my love of gardening.

My next find was a large, hand-forged spade shaped like a heart. Although made in the nineteenth century, it looked almost new. I hung it on the side of our barn like a piece of sculpture. Soon after, I brought home a few wrought-iron hand tools that have proved indispensable during my weeks of spring planting. I have since added countless trowels, pruners, and even a daisy grubber or two to my collection. Lately, I have been particularly interested in flower gatherers, which Victorians used to cut blooms from their conservatories.

When I first moved to Vermont, it was as if I had travelled to a faraway land, a land where the grocery store is an hour's drive away and the local newspaper is published monthly. But my new home introduced me to such things as country byways, backyard wildlife, and, of course, gardening. I may not have been born a gardener, but I am glad that life's unpredictable path led me to become one. Gardening helped me understand a strange new way of life far away from the city. My growing collection of garden tools is an expression of my love for that life, no longer strange, but comfortable and familiar.

Cultivating a Tool Collection

If you would like to collect antique gardening tools, here are some interesting facts:

This gathering of antique tools reflects the gardening style of yesteryear. Image from the book Antiques from the Garden *by Alistair Morris, published by Garden Art Press.*

History

• Until the sixteenth century, gardeners were limited to basic, heavy tools such as hoes and rakes, which had evolved from agricultural implements. By the middle of the next century, interest in gardening led to more innovative and useful tools, including hedging shears and trowels.

• Throughout the 1800s, iron gardening tools were often forged by local blacksmiths and constructed especially for their owners: an extra long hoe for a tall gardener, pruners for someone left-handed, or a small rake for a child.

• Tools were first produced in specific designs and finishes during the nineteenth century.

• Some popular tool designs were produced for a period of fifty years; therefore, dating tools can be difficult.

• Due to their quality construction and durability, many antique tools can be used in the garden today despite their age.

Purchasing

• Estate sales are excellent sources for finding tools. Search outbuildings or porches for tools that may have been overlooked.

• Although tools may cost only a few dollars at estate sales or flea markets, antique dealers or specialty garden shops may charge up to several hundred dollars per tool.

• Many hand-crafted tools were stamped with the name of the toolmaker, which offers a clue to the tool's origin.

Unique Finds

• A double-headed tool used to remove mistletoe from trees.

• Victorian wrought-iron spools for holding gardening twine.

• A rare implement which could be used to slice a stray weed or to putt a golf ball. It also can be used as a walking stick.

• Garden chests from the mid-1800s that contain a complete set of gardening tools.

Chart of Spring

Sylvia Trent Auxier

When my unquiet heart,
Forever voyaging,
Enjoined my pen to chart
A new design of spring,
I traced its facets many
As a jewel's fashioning.

I marked the tenderness
And warmth with which it wooed
The lifeless seed to press
Up through the soil, renewed:
And opened apple blossoms
To the sun's beatitude.

I traced the ecstasy
That trilled the redbird's note,
Billowed, exultingly,
The swamp frog's tawny throat,
Aroused the streams to laughter
And inflamed the pollen mote.

When my wayward heart
At last returned to me
And read the penciled chart,
The Spring's epitome,
My heart cried, "Spring? That's God."
And marvelled silently.

In Hollis, New Hampshire, the view through the branches of an apple tree reveals the flowering orchard beyond. Photograph by William Johnson/Johnson's Photography.

ONE • SEED

Mark Weinrich

From every opened flower,
the fragrance fresh,
One seed has shared its life
by facing death.
Beneath the soil its withered
form gave birth
And burst the earthy tomb
to garden light.

From wrinkled husks transformed
to verdant wings,
Spring's miracle of green,
a sacrifice.
And multitudes, amazed,
remember Christ—
One Seed has faced our death
to give us

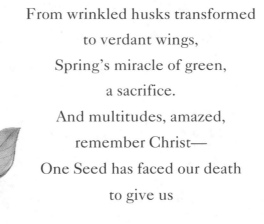

LIFE

A single lily of the valley stands among the greenery in Door County, Wisconsin. Photograph by Darryl Beers.

Mountains

Jessie Wilmore Murton

I think God must love mountains! For they seem
To hold so much of Him—such majesty
Of cliff and crag; such loveliness of stream
And cloud; such quiet strength of towering tree
And stone; their grandeur lent an airy grace
By distance and the sky's infinitude!
Where light and shade, in changing motif, trace
For beauty's creed each bright beatitude.

It may be, since their rugged heights upraise
So close to heaven, that they grow into
Some likeness to the beauty of that Face
Beyond the barrier of flawless blue—
Remembering, from ancient Sinai,
The cleft rock and Jehovah passing by!

Wildflowers adorn the Tatoosh Mountains in Mt. Rainier National Park in Washington.
Photograph by Dennis Frates/Oregon Scenics.

Always Easter

Grace V. Watkins

You say it happened long ago
And in a far-off land
Where men and women spoke a tongue
I would not understand,
That centuries have come and gone
Since that triumphant day,
And that the garden where He walked
Is half a world away.

He walks in every garden, friend;
And every rock-sealed tomb
Opens 'neath His shining hand
As springtime flowers bloom.
For every dawn is Easter dawn:
On every sunrise hill
The earthbound glimpse eternity
And meet the Master still.

Let us, then, plant with diligence and care the garden of the soil, but let us, with far deeper earnestness, tend the garden of our hearts.

—from *The Cottage Gardener*, 1849

The perfect place to enjoy a quiet garden is pictured in The Ornamental Seat *by artist Charles Neal. Image from Superstock.*

THROUGH MY WINDOW

Pamela Kennedy

Art by Stephanie Britt

"GOD'S FRIDAY"

Mary sighed and leaned her head back against the rough wall of her house. When the two distraught disciples had come rapping at her door with the news that Jesus had been arrested and taken to the high priest, she had wrapped herself in her shawl, suddenly chilled. After their departure, she sank down upon a small wooden bench near the doorway. Jesus had built the bench years ago when He was just a boy in Joseph's carpenter shop. She ran her fingers along its smooth edges, smiling slightly as she recalled His pride when He presented it to her. So many memories tumbled through her mind. She raised her eyes and watched the myriad stars shimmering in the black sky. They seemed to be spin-

ning, spiraling in the darkness, drawing her upward, upward and back in time to another night, long ago.

It was over three decades past, and she was a girl once more. Alone on the rooftop of her parents' home, she sat and gazed at the stars above Nazareth, dreaming of her marriage to Joseph. And then the angel Gabriel appeared with his astonishing news. She remembered his every word and now quietly repeated her response: "I am the Lord's servant. May it be to me as you have said."

She recalled a star-filled night in Bethlehem less than a year later when the angel's promise was fulfilled and Jesus was born. The joy of that evening was soon overshadowed by another, darker night. By pale starlight, Joseph, she, and the baby had fled Herod's wrath, running for their lives through

Sinai's wild desert toward the safety of Egypt.

So many nights, some filled with wonder, others with pain, had passed since then. She closed her eyes and sighed once more. What would this night bring? She did not fear the darkness, for she had learned long ago that God is light and in Him is no darkness. But she also knew that men preferred their own darkness to God's light. Where was her Son now? Into what darkness had they taken Him? She remembered the song she sang long ago as she shared Gabriel's news with Elisabeth.

"My soul praises the Lord and my spirit rejoices in God my Saviour, for he has been mindful of the humble state of his servant. From now on all generations will call me blessed, for the mighty one has done great things for me—holy is his name" (Luke 1:46–49).

She opened her eyes and looked into the vastness of the night. The Lord's greatness and blessings were both precious and painful, yet she would not have traded a moment of her life for that of another. And now, the Lord was asking her to walk with Him in a new path. As if reaching out in obedience once again, she lifted her hand toward the heavens and whispered, "I am the Lord's servant."

She sat thus, still as a statue, until the pale shimmer of dawn crept over the hilltops and pushed its way slowly into her awareness. In the shadowed street she glimpsed a woman hurrying toward her.

"Mary!" the woman called, and Mary recognized the voice of her sister. Standing, she received the wife of Cleophas with a warm embrace. "They've taken Jesus and held a mockery of a trial," her sister gasped between breaths. She wrung her hands and continued, "Even now they are dragging Him before Pilate, begging for His crucifixion! Do you think we should go to Him?"

Mary stiffened as if pierced with a sword and grasped the other woman's hand. "We will remain here and pray. The Lord will tell us what we should do. Come, dear sister." Quietly they went inside and knelt together on the hard floor.

They were there when the Apostle John came to the house hours later with the dreadful news. The time had come. Quickly they pulled their shawls over their heads and hurried with him to Golgotha.

Mary stood in the midst of the crowd, yet she felt alone, staring at her oldest Son. She recalled His first steps, His first words, the way He ran to show her the precise symmetry of a butterfly's wing, or the smooth-grained beauty of a well-made table. Her love silently reached out to Him above the din of the shouting crowd, and He slowly turned His head as if in response to the cry of her heart. She raised her arms toward Him and caught His eyes with her own. It was as if her grieving soul calmed in that moment. Time stopped, and all the fragments of the past thirty-three years fell into place: the annunciation, the prophetic words of Anna and Simeon, the escape and return from Egypt, the words Jesus spoke in the temple when He was only twelve, His teaching and miracles, His prayers and healings. These and thousands of other words and images suddenly coincided in an eternal tapestry, and Mary realized the truth. This execution on a barren Judean hillside was no accident of evil perpetrated by mere men. In that moment Mary saw the fulfillment of God's perfect plan. Through the sacrifice of Christ's death would come the long-promised hope of everlasting life. When she had spoken her own words of obedience as a girl, she had not known all that they would mean. But when she heard Jesus say, "Father, into your hands I commit my spirit," she understood the price of commitment.

When the terrible darkness of the afternoon lifted and the figures on the three crosses were still, Mary allowed the Apostle John to lead her gently down the hillside to her home. She assured him she would be fine and urged him to go comfort the others. That night she sat again on the bench Jesus had made as a boy, looking out at the shimmering stars, knowing what the others would soon discover. This day was not an ending but a beginning. She leaned back against the wall of the house and closed her eyes. Her fingers slowly traced the straight, smooth edge of the bench her Son had made, and she smiled as she drifted into sleep.

Pamela Kennedy is a freelance writer of short stories, articles, essays, and children's books. Wife of a retired naval office and mother of three children, she has made her home on both U.S. coasts and currently resides in Honolulu, Hawaii.

The Entry into Jerusalem

And when they came nigh to Jerusalem, unto Bethphage and Bethany, at the mount of Olives, he sendeth forth two of his disciples, And saith unto them, Go your way into the village over against you: and as soon as ye be entered into it, ye shall find a colt tied, whereon never man sat; loose him, and bring him. And if any man say unto you, Why do ye this? say ye that the Lord hath need of him; and straightway he will send him hither. And they went their way, and found the colt tied by the door without in a place where two ways met; and they loose him. And certain of them that stood there said unto them, What do ye, loosing the colt? And they said unto them even as Jesus had commanded: and they let them go.

And they brought the colt to Jesus, and cast their garments on him; and he sat upon him. And many spread their garments in the way: and others cut down branches off the trees, and strawed them in the way. And they that went before, and they that followed, cried, saying, Hosanna; Blessed is he that cometh in the name of the Lord: Blessed be the kingdom of our father David, that cometh in the name of the Lord: Hosanna in the highest.

And Jesus entered into Jerusalem, and into the temple: and when he had looked round about upon all things, and now the eventide was come, he went out unto Bethany with the twelve.

Mark 11:1–11

Entry into Jerusalem by artist Giotto di Bondone (1266–1337). Image from Scrovegni Chapel, Padua, Italy/Alinari/Art Resource, New York.

The Betrayal

And he came out, and went, as he was wont, to the mount of Olives; and his disciples also followed him. And when he was at the place, he said unto them, Pray that ye enter not into temptation. And he was withdrawn from them about a stone's cast, and kneeled down, and prayed, Saying, Father, if thou be willing, remove this cup from me: nevertheless not my will, but thine, be done.

And while he yet spake, behold a multitude, and he that was called Judas, one of the twelve, went before them, and drew near unto Jesus to kiss him. But Jesus said unto him, Judas, betrayest thou the Son of man with a kiss?

When they which were about him saw what would follow, they said unto him, Lord, shall we smite with the sword? And one of them smote the servant of the high priest, and cut off his right ear. And Jesus answered and said, Suffer ye thus far. And he touched his ear, and healed him.

Then Jesus said unto the chief priests, and captains of the temple, and the elders, which were come to him, Be ye come out, as against a thief, with swords and staves? When I was daily with you in the temple, ye stretched forth no hands against me: but this is your hour, and the power of darkness.

Then took they him, and led him, and brought him into the high priest's house. And Peter followed afar off.

Luke 22:39–42; 47–54

The Betrayal of Christ by artist Giotto di Bondone (1266–1337). Image from Arena Chapel, Cappella Degli Scrovegni, Padua, Italy/Superstock.

The Way of the Cross

Then came Jesus forth, wearing the crown of thorns, and the purple robe. And Pilate saith unto them, Behold the man! When the chief priests therefore and officers saw him, they cried out, saying, Crucify him, crucify him. Pilate saith unto them, Take ye him, and crucify him: for I find no fault in him. The Jews answered him, We have a law, and by our law he ought to die, because he made himself the Son of God. When Pilate therefore heard that saying, he was the more afraid; And went again into the judgment hall, and saith unto Jesus, Whence art thou? But Jesus gave him no answer. Then saith Pilate unto him, Speakest thou not unto me? knowest thou not that I have power to crucify thee, and have power to release thee? Jesus answered, Thou couldest have no power at all against me, except it were given thee from above: therefore he that delivered me unto thee hath the greater sin.

And from thenceforth Pilate sought to release him: but the Jews cried out, saying, If thou let this man go, thou art not Caesar's friend: whosoever maketh himself a king speaketh against Caesar. When Pilate therefore heard that saying, he brought Jesus forth, and sat down in the judgment seat in a place that is called the Pavement, but in the Hebrew, Gabbatha.

Then delivered he him therefore unto them to be crucified. And they took Jesus, and led him away. And he bearing his cross went forth into a place called the place of a skull, which is called in the Hebrew Golgotha.

John 19:5–13, 16, 17

Christ Carrying the Cross by artist Giotto di Bondone (1266–1337). Image from Arena Chapel, Cappella Degli Scrovegni, Padua, Italy/Superstock.

The Crucifixion

And when they were come unto a place called Golgotha, that is to say, a place of a skull, They gave him vinegar to drink mingled with gall: and when he had tasted thereof, he would not drink. And they crucified him, and parted his garments, casting lots: that it might be fulfilled which was spoken by the prophet, They parted my garments among them, and upon my vesture did they cast lots.

And sitting down they watched him there; And set up over his head his accusation written, THIS IS JESUS THE KING OF THE JEWS. Then were there two thieves crucified with him, one on the right hand, and another on the left.

And they that passed by reviled him, wagging their heads, And saying, Thou that destroyest the temple, and buildest it in three days, save thyself. If thou be the Son of God, come down from the cross. Likewise also the chief priests mocking him, with the scribes and elders, said, He saved others; himself he cannot save. If he be the King of Israel, let him now come down from the cross, and we will believe him. He trusted in God; let him deliver him now, if he will have him: for he said, I am the Son of God.

And about the ninth hour Jesus cried with a loud voice, saying, Eli, Eli, lama sabachthani? that is to say, My God, my God, why hast thou forsaken me? Jesus, when he had cried again with a loud voice, yielded up the ghost.

Matthew 27:33–43, 46, 50

Crucifixion by artist Giotto di Bondone (1266–1337). Image from Arena Chapel, Cappella Degli Scrovegni, Padua, Italy/Superstock.

The Resurrection

But Mary stood without at the sepulchre weeping: and as she wept, she stooped down, and looked into the sepulchre, And seeth two angels in white sitting, the one at the head, and the other at the feet, where the body of Jesus had lain. And they say unto her, Woman, why weepest thou? She saith unto them, Because they have taken away my Lord, and I know not where they have laid him.

And when she had thus said, she turned herself back, and saw Jesus standing, and knew not that it was Jesus. Jesus saith unto her, Woman, why weepest thou? whom seekest thou? She, supposing him to be the gardener, saith unto him, Sir, if thou have borne him hence, tell me where thou hast laid him, and I will take him away.

Jesus saith unto her, Mary. She turned herself, and saith unto him, Rabboni; which is to say, Master. Jesus saith unto her, Touch me not; for I am not yet ascended to my Father: but go to my brethren, and say unto them, I ascend unto my Father, and your Father; and to my God, and your God.

John 20:11–17

Touch Me Not by artist Giotto di Bondone (1266–1337). Image from Arena Chapel, Cappella Degli Scrovegni, Padua, Italy/Superstock.

The Ascension

And he said unto them, These are the words which I spake unto you, while I was yet with you, that all things must be fulfilled, which were written in the law of Moses, and in the prophets, and in the psalms, concerning me. Then opened he their understanding, that they might understand the scriptures, And said unto them, Thus it is written, and thus it behoved Christ to suffer, and to rise from the dead the third day: And that repentance and remission of sins should be preached in his name among all nations, beginning at Jerusalem. And ye are witnesses of these things. And, behold, I send the promise of my Father upon you: but tarry ye in the city of Jerusalem, until ye be endued with power from on high.

And he led them out as far as to Bethany, and he lifted up his hands, and blessed them. And it came to pass, while he blessed them, he was parted from them, and carried up into heaven. And they worshipped him, and returned to Jerusalem with great joy: And were continually in the temple, praising and blessing God. Amen.

Luke 24:44–53

The Ascension *by artist Giotto di Bondone (1266–1337). Image from Arena Chapel, Cappella Degli Scrovegni, Padua, Italy/Superstock.*

Devotions FROM THE Heart

Pamela Kennedy

"Jesus saith unto him, Thomas, because thou hast seen me, thou hast believed: blessed are they that have not seen, and yet have believed." John 20:29

WALKING IN FAITH

When we experience sorrow or grief and cannot see the way ahead, what keeps us going? It is not the ability to see or touch a brighter day, but a belief that although we exist in darkness, the light will return; it is faith that looks beyond the present reality to a future as yet unrevealed.

With telescopes in outer space, spy satellites circling the globe, and electron microscopes penetrating the core of the atom, it would seem logical to assume that if we can't see it, it must not exist. Life, however, consists of so much more than the material universe, whether large or small.

Hold a newborn child and consider the potential resting in your arms. You can neither see nor touch the talents, gifts, and intellect residing in her, yet what parent refuses to believe they exist? We encourage and teach and train in order to nurture the hidden gifts residing in each child. It is the belief in the unseen that drives us on.

In the Easter story, amid the glad tidings of the Resurrection, Thomas stands in lonely grief. Because he was absent when Jesus appeared to the other disciples, he missed an opportunity to experience the resurrected Lord. When confronted with their story of seeing Christ, Thomas adamantly refused to believe it. He claimed he would not even believe if he did see it! Only if he were able to touch the risen Lord, to place his own fingers in the wounded side and hands, only then would he consider believing the resurrection. Yet how many of us wander in that same wilderness of hopelessness, not because the truth doesn't exist, but because we cannot see it and therefore refuse to accept it?

Blinded by loneliness, we cannot see the faces of those around us who would offer comfort, and so we believe there is no comfort. Wounded by one we trusted, we see only betrayal and resist the love offered by another. Caught in the darkness of anxiety, we experience fear and worry, ignoring the light of hope and faith. When only seeing is believing, our options are severely limited; our blessings few.

How gracious God is to reveal the end of Thomas's story of blinded faith. Jesus comes face to face with Thomas and invites him to explore the reality of the Resurrection with his own hands. Thus confronted, Thomas's pride crumbles and he falls, worshiping at his Messiah's feet. It is then that Christ utters the gentle rebuke that reveals a great truth: "Thomas, because thou has seen me, thou hast believed: blessed are they that have not seen, and yet have believed."

Our faith rests not in sight. Who has ever seen the properties of a prayer, the process of anguish turned to peace, the chemical components involved in the healing of a tormented

God, I thank You for the blessings of Your Resurrection that demonstrate the unseen power of Your love. Help me to walk this day by faith, enlightened by Your vision, not my own.

Artist Roberto Ferruzzi captures the trusting nature of a young child in his painting entitled Girl. Image from the Pushkin Museum of Fine Arts, Moscow, Russia/Superstock.

soul? Who can understand the miracle of a healed marriage, the lifting of a heavy heart, the restoration of a wayward child? Yet all these things happen around us every day. They are a testimony to the power of the unseen God and the abundant blessing of unmeasured grace. When we reach the end of our own understanding and give up our insistence for positive proof, then we are able to experience the inexplicable joy of a faith that is not limited by sight.

When It Is Easter

Helen Harrington

It is Easter now that hills
Are adorned with daffodils,
Now that ivory lilies grace
The garden pot and altar vase.

It is Easter now that spires
Shine with sunlight, now that choirs
Sing "Hallelujah!" and we come
In the faith of Christendom,

Believing love is twice as great
As suspicion, fear, and hate,
That the stony, angry door
Opens up to trust once more,

Believing too, that when we find
Joy supreme in being kind
And acknowledge peace sublime,
It is truly Eastertime!

*A church in Bridgewater, Connecticut, awaits its Easter Sunday visitors. Photograph
by William Johnson/Johnson's Photography.*

On Easter Morning

Kathryn Stephenson Wilhelm

Tulips marching, two by two,
On stately stems in brilliant hue.

Children marching, two by four,
Marching through the front church door,
Dressed in tulips' brilliant hues
To brighten somber, stately pews.

Easter Sunday Cherub

Marian Paust

Caught by the glamour
Of her Easter gown,
She walks sedately
With her head bent down.

Her eyes follow closely
The quick come and go
Of each new gleaming
Patent leather toe.

Dressed in their Easter finery, two young girls prepare for an after-church egg hunt. Photograph by Superstock.

Easter Outlook

Inez Franck

I view the earth adorned in snowflake plum,
The bluebells ringing down the garden rows,
And everywhere is live with robin song,
The verdant country fields that spring bestows.
The little streams come by with woodland glee,
The hyacinths are dancing in the sun;
The world awakes to miracles of love
And tells a message clear for everyone.

I think this loveliness unfolds a plan.
It is God's way of speaking to my heart
And showing life with great expectancy—
The living hope that Easter scenes impart.
The Resurrection glory fills these hours
With songs of joy that only He can give;
I look to Easter's everlasting light
And feel because He lives I too shall live.

Hyacinths form a purple carpet at the Keukenhof Gardens in Lisse, Holland. Photograph by Robert Reiff/FPG International.

An Easter lily announces spring's arrival. Photograph by Norman Poole.

Easter Lilies

Sudie Stuart Hager

I did not see the rock-hewn vault
Where Christ, my Lord, lay dead
Nor scent the precious sweet perfume
They poured upon His head.
I did not see the ponderous stone
The angel rolled away

Nor hear His kind assuring voice
On Resurrection day.
But I have seen His robe that shone
In Easter's pale dawn light,
For He has clothed His lilies here
In angel-drapery white.

A rare triple trillium stands out brilliantly against its dark foliage. Photograph by Dick Luria/FPG International.

Softly Praising

Cecile Houghton Stury

Once more among the hills
  has glory come,
Attended by a million trillium
Full-patterned in the name of trinity.

With leafy hand and lip and heart I see
Them sing—this white-robed,
  reverent lily host—
Softly praising Father, Son,
  and Holy Ghost.

From My Garden Journal

by Deana Deck

My grandmother's best friend was a sweet lady named Mrs. LaFoon. Hers was not a common name, so it always stuck in my memory. What I remember even more about Mrs. LaFoon, however, was her collection of cute, colorful hens and chickens. These weren't the actual birds, and they weren't the plants by the same name either; they were ceramic dishes, shaped like chickens of all sizes with a top half that lifted off.

What was truly wonderful about the ceramic birds, from a child's point of view, was that they were always filled with special goodies. One might contain peanuts or cashews, whereas others held raisins or jelly beans or melt-in-your-mouth dinner mints. When my grandmother took me along on visits, Mrs. LaFoon would let me choose a chicken and enjoy a handful of the treats I found inside. My favorite was a red, blue, and yellow rooster that held Mrs. LaFoon's delicious honey-roasted pecans.

The little rock-

garden plant called hens-and-chickens always makes me think of the flock of porcelain poultry in Mrs. LaFoon's glass-front china cabinet. Judging from a discovery I made recently while researching a question about succulents, someone else has made the same connection. I stumbled across a photo of a wall shelf decorated with an assortment of green ceramic hens and little rosettes of the hens-and-chickens plant. Combining the two in a decorative arrangement seems such an obvious thing to do; I'm surprised that I never thought of it before! What a great idea for a festive holiday table setting, especially for a spring celebration like Easter.

One of the things that caught my eye about the photo was the caption. It referred to the hens-and-chickens plant as a member of the *Echeveria x imbricata* species. These plants are true succulents and are native to dry desert regions where the ability to store water in plant tissue for long periods of time is essential for survival.

When I began researching the hens-and-chickens plant, however, I was surprised to find that there are actually two types—the desert *Echeveria* species (which was pictured in the photo I had found), and the more common *Sempervirens tectorum* species. Although the two types are similar in appearance, they are quite different. Whereas the *Echeveria* species grows in the desert, the *Sempervirens* species belongs to the large family of stonecrops or sedums and thrives in temperate

HENS AND CHICKENS

zones, including much of North America, Eastern Europe, and the mountainous regions of the Middle East.

The *Sempervirens tectorum* originated in Eastern Europe, where it often grows on house-tops and is called the common (or foot) house-leek. Since this common hens-and-chickens plant in no way resembles the mild, onion-like leek used in cookery, this part of its name remains a mystery I will probably continue to try solving. Nevertheless, here's what you need to know about growing the common hens-and-chickens plant in your garden.

Hens-and-chickens look rather like open artichokes, but with fatter leaves. They are not difficult to grow and in many climates are extremely hardy. Because they hug the ground and have shallow roots, they are ideal plants for the rock garden or for containers. They are prolific breeders and if left alone will form a dense mat-like clump of plants.

The plant's nickname is derived from its habit of propagation. Each mature plant, or "hen," produces offsets or baby plants that resemble a little flock of "chicks" around its perimeter. These offsets can be left to cover a wide area or can be transplanted to other parts of the garden, given to friends, or potted in containers for use indoors.

The plants are very hardy and can be grown from seed if it is available, although many plants grown from seed do not bloom as well as those derived from offsets. Blooms are usually yellow, although some varieties produce a small pink bloom. However, it is the foliage, rather than the bloom, that is the plant's major attraction. The mature plants are green, but leaf tips can vary in color, depending on the variety. Colors can range through various shades of bronze-red to maroon and purple.

Care of hens-and-chickens is similar to that of other sedums. When brought indoors, they prefer bright light; but outdoor plants thrive in partial shade. They can tolerate cold, but do best when mulched in winter and protected from drying winds. They are very tolerant of high humidity.

Sedums have shallow root systems, so garden soil should drain well; and because they store water in their leaves, it's best to let the soil approach dryness between waterings to avoid damping off. When growing sedums in containers, use a gritty, somewhat sandy soil. I've found that the type of soil sold for cactus plants is an ideal choice. Also, clay pots, which drain well, are preferable to plastic containers.

For use in a table arrangement for Easter Sunday dinner, the hens-and-chickens rosettes can be temporarily repotted in shallow clay saucers and set on a tray or basket of colorful Easter eggs. Or, as Mrs. LaFoon might have done (had she been familiar with the plant), set them in among a collection of china hens and chickens. At Easter, however, you may want to add a bunny or two!

Deana Deck tends her flowers, plants, and vegetables at her home in Nashville, Tennessee, where her popular garden column is a regular feature in The Tennessean.

Each mature plant, or "hen," produces offsets or baby plants that resemble a little flock of "chicks" around its perimeter.

In Tulip Time

Mary H. Beam

Secure and warmly sheltered
By my misty windowpane,
I marvel at the fury
Of the springtime wind and rain.

The garden paths are littered
With the wreckage of the gale—
Young leaves and buds and blossoms,
Hapless victims of the hail.

But there, with stems unbroken,
Though by winds lashed to and fro,
Their rainbow colors gleaming,
Are the tulips, row on row.

As ships on stormy oceans
Can survive a furious blast
By keeping all their canvas
Snugly furled against the mast,

Just so my valiant tulips,
In their stormy springtime world,
Are weathering out this tempest
With their petals tightly curled.

I wonder how my tulips
Learned this wisdom seamen know?
If winds become unfriendly,
Trim your sails and let them blow.

*Above: Raindrops gather on a single crimson tulip. Photograph by
William Johnson/Johnson's Photography.
Left: A field of tulips offers a kaleidoscope of color in Marion County,
Oregon. Photograph by Steve Terrill.*

For Water

Violet Alleyn Storey

God, for each guise of water, praise to Thee!
For flower-loved streams whose silver mirrors hold
The night's starred darkness and the day's blue-gold.
Our thanks for wave-rhymed silences of sea,
For fountains, too, whose slender shuttles weave
Cool veils to shield the garden's sun-flushed face,
For rivers rising in some far, strange place,
For inland pools that summer showers leave!
Our thanks for wells such as Rebekah knew,
For gay, untutored rain that tumbles down,
For dew that lies like some frail, lacy gown,
For lakes like that near which the Christ Child grew!
And thanks, kind God, that, when we pause to sup,
Thou givest us clear water in a cup.

"I've got peace like a river; I've got joy like a fountain in my soul."

–Traditional spiritual

Daffodils frame a fountain at Sister Bay in Wisconsin. Photograph by Darryl Beers.

OUR HERITAGE

FROM THE OPENING ADDRESS OF THE NATIONAL CONFERENCE ON CONSERVATION, 1908

This conference on the conservation of natural resources is, in effect, a meeting of the representatives of all the people of the United States called to consider the weightiest problem now before the Nation; and the occasion for the meeting lies in the fact that the natural resources of our country are in danger of exhaustion if we permit the old wasteful methods of exploiting them longer to continue. . . .

The wise use of all of our natural resources, which are our national resources as well, is the great material question of today. I have asked you to come together now because the enormous consumption of these resources, and the threat of imminent exhaustion of some of them, due to reckless and wasteful use, . . . calls for common effort, common action. . . .

It is safe to say that the prosperity of our people depends directly on the energy and intelligence with which our natural resources are used. It is equally clear that these resources are the final basis of national power and perpetuity. Finally, it is ominously evident that these resources are in the course of rapid exhaustion. . . .

We have become great in a material sense because of the lavish use of our resources, and we have just reason to be proud of our growth. But the time has come to inquire seriously what will happen when our forests are gone, when the coal, the iron, the oil, and the gas are exhausted, when the soils shall have been still further impoverished and washed into the streams, polluting the rivers, denuding the fields, and obstructing navigation. These questions do not relate only to the next century or to the next generation. One distinguishing characteristic of really civilized men is foresight; we have to, as a nation, exercise foresight for this nation in the future; and if we do not exercise that foresight, dark will be the future!

Theodore Roosevelt

ABOUT THE TEXT

In the early days of the conservation movement, Theodore Roosevelt was crucial in leading the fight. During his presidency, he encouraged the federal government to acquire and protect two hundred million acres of public land and to establish five new national parks. In the spring of 1908, Roosevelt organized a national conference on conservation for one thousand participants, including governors, Congressmen, and scientists. The conference served as a turning point in conservation history and established the protection of America's natural resources as an important national issue.

Phantom Ship Island can be seen through the frame of a twisted branch at Crater Lake National Park in Oregon, one of the national parks established by Theodore Roosevelt. Photograph by Dennis Frates/Oregon Scenics.

Easter in the Woods

Frances Frost

This dawn when the mountain cherry lifts
Its frail white bloom among dark pines,
And chipmunks flash small happy paws
Along old tumbled boundary lines,
This golden morning when the vixen
Nuzzles her five young foxes forth
To roll in ferns in the Easter sun,
Again the woods know soft green birth.

Snuffed by a puffball infant rabbit
Are yellow violets by the spring;
Among half-opened apple buds
A wood thrush tilts its head to sing.
Risen is He! And they are His,
Who scamper under warm blue skies,
Who nibble little fists of grass,
And gaze on earth with shy glad eyes.

Above: An eastern cottontail bunny is caught nibbling a tasty bit of clover. Photograph by Gay Bumgarner.
Left: Silver dollar wildflowers line a trail through Oregon's Columbia River Gorge National Scenic Area. Photograph by Steve Terrill.

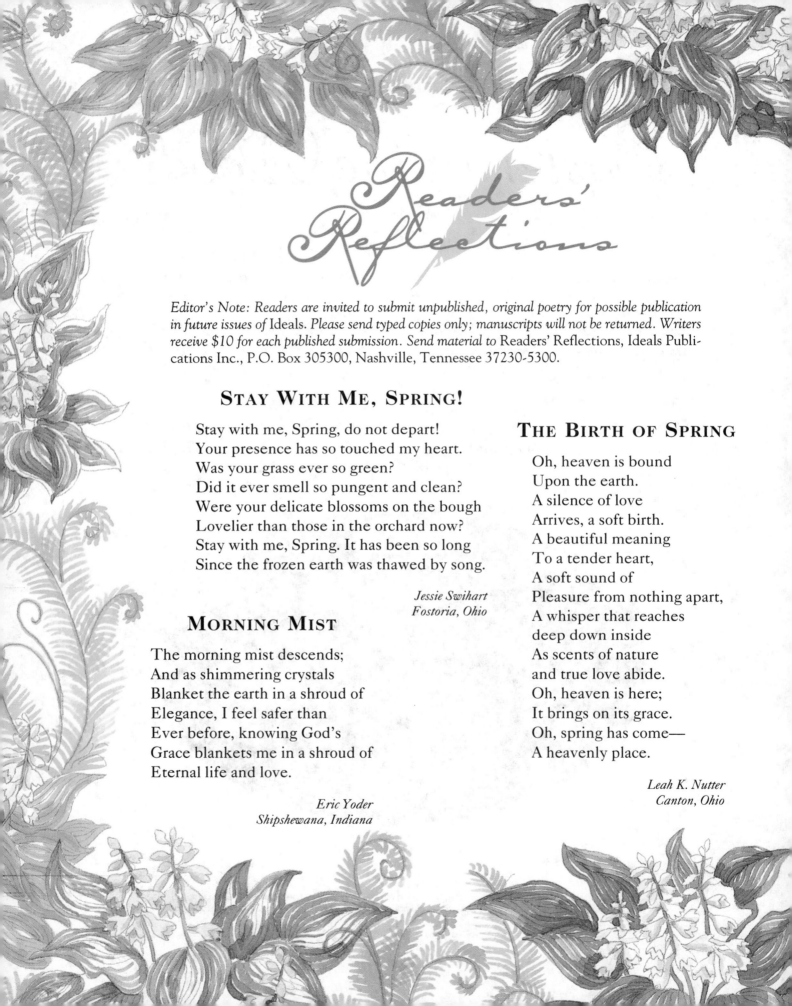

Readers' Reflections

Editor's Note: Readers are invited to submit unpublished, original poetry for possible publication in future issues of Ideals. *Please send typed copies only; manuscripts will not be returned. Writers receive $10 for each published submission. Send material to Readers' Reflections, Ideals Publications Inc., P.O. Box 305300, Nashville, Tennessee 37230-5300.*

STAY WITH ME, SPRING!

Stay with me, Spring, do not depart!
Your presence has so touched my heart.
Was your grass ever so green?
Did it ever smell so pungent and clean?
Were your delicate blossoms on the bough
Lovelier than those in the orchard now?
Stay with me, Spring. It has been so long
Since the frozen earth was thawed by song.

Jessie Swihart
Fostoria, Ohio

MORNING MIST

The morning mist descends;
And as shimmering crystals
Blanket the earth in a shroud of
Elegance, I feel safer than
Ever before, knowing God's
Grace blankets me in a shroud of
Eternal life and love.

Eric Yoder
Shipshewana, Indiana

THE BIRTH OF SPRING

Oh, heaven is bound
Upon the earth.
A silence of love
Arrives, a soft birth.
A beautiful meaning
To a tender heart,
A soft sound of
Pleasure from nothing apart,
A whisper that reaches
deep down inside
As scents of nature
and true love abide.
Oh, heaven is here;
It brings on its grace.
Oh, spring has come—
A heavenly place.

Leah K. Nutter
Canton, Ohio

Springtime

It's springtime in the woodlands.
Each leaf with gossamer sheen
Is dressed in minted colors,
Pale yellow, gray, soft green.

Those fragile leaves, so tender,
Resembling fairy wing,
Will soon be strong and sturdy
When it's no longer spring.

And then with summer's passing
The gorgeous leaves of fall,
Stroked by a master Artist,
Will color one and all.

With snows of chill December,
Each barren twig agleam
Becomes a thing of beauty,
God's miracle supreme.

So true to life these seasons.
Swift passing time is seen
In infant, youth, adulthood,
Finally, old age, serene.

And when our years are over
In God's eternal plan,
We'll wake again to springtime
In some far, beauteous land.

Thelma Lee Cottrell
Pompano Beach, Florida

An Awakening

The earth stirs;
Upheaval begins,
Warmed by sun and rain,
Shifted by March winds.

Winter storms are over,
Another cycle takes place;
Nature sheds its frown
And puts on a smiling face!

One bright springtime morning
As the sun shines overhead,
Terra firma cracks open
As a crocus shows its head!

Gertrude Dunham
Bloomfield, New Jersey

Come Softly, Sweet Spring

Come softly, sweet Spring,
Cast your dainties abroad;
Let the seedlings spring forth
From the rich earthen sod.
Sweet maiden awake
To the sound of the lute,
And put on your garments
And wildflower suit.

Pam Iseley
Greensboro, North Carolina

There is perhaps no better writer to describe Florida's Everglades than Marjory Stoneman Douglas, whose lifelong efforts helped save this national treasure. In the following excerpt from her award-winning book, Douglas shares the many wonders of this diverse region.

FROM THE EVERGLADES: RIVER OF GRASS

Marjory Stoneman Douglas

There are no other Everglades in the world. They are, they have always been, one of the unique regions of the earth, remote, never wholly known. Nothing anywhere else is like them: their vast glittering openness, wider than the enormous visible round of the horizon, the racing free saltness and sweetness of their massive winds, under the dazzling blue heights of space. They are unique also in the simplicity, the diversity, the related harmony of the forms of life they enclose. The miracle of the light pours over the green and brown expanse of saw grass and of water, shining and slow-moving below, the grass and water that is the meaning and the central fact of the Everglades of Florida. It is a river of grass. . . .

Over the shallows, often less than a foot deep but seven hundred fifty or so square miles in actual area, the winds in one gray swift moment can shatter the reflections of sky and cloud whiteness standing still in that shining, polished, shimmering expanse. A boat can push for hours in a day of white sun through the short, crisp lake waves and there will be nothing to be seen anywhere but the brightness where the color of the water and the color of the sky become one. Men out of sight of land can stand in it up to their armpits and slowly "walk in" their long nets to the waiting boats. An everglade kite and his mate, questing in great solitary circles, rising and dipping and rising again on the wind currents, can look down all day long at the water faintly green with floating water lettuce or marked by thin standing lines of reeds, utter their sharp goat cries, and be seen and heard by no one at all. . . .

It reaches one hundred miles from Lake Okeechobee to the Gulf of Mexico, fifty, sixty, even seventy miles wide. No one has ever fought his way along its full length. Few have ever crossed the northern wilderness of nothing but grass. Down that almost invisible slope the water moves. The grass stands. Where the grass and the water are there is the heart, the current, the meaning of the Everglades.

The grass and the water together make the river as simple as it is unique. There is no other river like it. Yet within that simplicity, enclosed within the river and bordering and intruding on it from each side, there is subtlety and diversity, a crowd of changing forms, of thrusting teeming life. And all that becomes the region of the Everglades.

Slash pines and palmettos fill the landscape in this portion of The Everglades. Photograph by Stan Osolinski/FPG International.

LEGENDARY AMERICANS

MICHELLE PRATER BURKE

MARJORY STONEMAN DOUGLAS

Marjory Stoneman Douglas once said, "Every life is lived all along the way in bits and pieces that assemble into one's story." Douglas believed in making every piece and every day count, and, in doing so, she lived a remarkable life that lasted over a century. From an ordinary yet troubled childhood, she built a life of extraordinary accomplishments, all of which led her to her life's crusade: saving Florida's Everglades.

Marjory Stoneman was born in Minneapolis on April 7, 1890, to parents Frank and Lillian Stoneman. Her father's family traced its roots to the Quakers, to whom Douglas later attributed her early sense of "independence and pigheadedness." The family moved to Providence, Rhode Island, when Marjory Stoneman was three; and her early child-

hood there was peaceful, filled with memories of reading with her father and taking long nature walks with her beloved mother.

But Frank Stoneman experienced repeated business failures, and the stress took its toll on his wife, who suffered a mental breakdown. The couple separated when their daughter was only six, and Marjory and her mother left to live with Lillian's parents in Taunton, Massachusetts. Books became the child's escape from the difficult family problems that surrounded her. Douglas later said the "dislocation of my life, being the child of a broken family" led her to question everything she was told.

Although reluctant to leave her ailing mother, Marjory Stoneman left for Wellesley College in the fall of 1908. At school, she discovered not only a freedom she had theretofore been unable to enjoy, but a talent for speaking and writing as well. Classes in what was then called "expression" taught her the public speaking skills she would use later in life. In English class, her first assignment was a letter describing the beauty of the oak trees on the campus. Her letter garnered applause from her classmates and immediately established her reputation as a writer.

Yet college left Douglas with little direction or plans for the future. After her mother's death from cancer, the daughter described herself as "completely lonely." She married Kenneth Douglas, a man thirty years her senior. Because of her husband's illegal business practices, she left him in September of 1915. Twenty-five years old, Marjory Stoneman Douglas moved to Florida to be reunited with her father, whom she had not seen since the age of six. She later recalled, "I left my marriage and all my past history without a single regret. I was heading south with a sense of release, excitement, and anticipation."

Douglas had first visited the South with her parents when she was only four. Her earliest memory of Florida was of being lifted up to pick an orange off a tree. Returning as an adult, she would discover journalism instead of oranges. Douglas's new career in journalism was due to her father, who was the first editor of the paper that later became the *Miami Herald*. Douglas began working for her father's paper, often writing about the issues that affected

Florida. After the start of World War I, she was sent to write an article on the first woman in Florida to enlist in the military. Douglas ended up becoming that woman herself by enlisting in the Navy, and she spent several years involved in relief work overseas before returning to Florida.

In 1926, Douglas built a tiny, Tudor-style cottage in Coconut Grove, Florida, where she would live alone for the rest of her long life. Yet Douglas enjoyed her own company and had no time to be lonely. After leaving the newspaper business, she began a successful fifteen-year career as a short-story writer for several national magazines. Yet her most ambitious projects were still to come.

In the early 1940s, a book publisher and friend, Hervey Allen, approached Douglas with the opportunity to write a book about the Miami River for a series on America's rivers. Douglas replied, "You can't write a book about the Miami River. It's only about an inch long," and she suggested a book about The Everglades instead. On that whim, Marjory Stoneman Douglas's connection with The Everglades began.

For years, landowners and developers had tried to drain and destroy the wetlands of Florida's Everglades. But where others saw only a swamp, Douglas saw much more. She realized that this vast sheet of water was moving, however slowly. She saw a river of grass, as had the Native American tribes of Southern Florida, who had called the area *Pahayokee*, meaning "grassy water." Douglas used her position as an author to educate others about this fragile network of water, weather, and wildlife, and to stress the importance of its protection.

In 1947, the same year President Harry Truman formally opened The Everglades National Park, Douglas published *The Everglades: River of Grass*. The book became a bestseller and introduced the world to the beauty and complexity of The Everglades. The book's lyrical descriptions of the landscapes and wildlife of the region caused the book to continue to sell ten thousand copies a year, even forty years after it was first published.

It was twenty years after publishing *River of Grass* that Douglas, at the age of seventy-eight, became an active environmentalist. The national park protected only a portion of The Everglades, and that portion was still adversely affected by the poor treatment of wildlife and water supplies outside it. Although her book did much to publicize the area's threatened condition, Douglas realized that mere words were not enough to protect The Everglades. With each passing year, more water and grass were being removed to make room for farms and ranches. In 1969, when developers began planning the construction of a jetport within the swamplands, Douglas realized the project would disturb the animal habitats and threaten the subtly balanced water systems of the region.

Spurred to action, she formed The Friends of The Everglades, a conservation group that would fight to preserve the area and work to save it from development, particularly from the planned jetport. As the outspoken leader of the group, Douglas began speaking to any organization that would listen. Within two years, the organization had more than one thousand members from thirty-eight states, and "Marjory's Army" (as they became known) had successfully blocked the construction of the airport.

During the last thirty years of her life, Douglas became the "Grandmother of the Glades" and fought to reestablish and protect the region's subtle balance of nature. She had always been a fighter, but until then had not found a cause worth fighting for. "It was almost as if the Everglades had waited for me," she said. Hers was not a glamorous job. The tiny, aged woman (wearing the ever-present large glasses and floppy hat) often spoke in crowded, hot, mosquito-filled gymnasiums, her sobering voice demanding the attention of angry landowners and planning committees.

Although Marjory Stoneman Douglas eventually lost her sight, her voice never failed her, and she became known by some as the Voice of The Everglades. She never considered her crusade to preserve The Everglades complete, and until her death in May 1998 at the remarkable age of 108, she was still fighting. Her long life took many turns along the way, but Douglas felt each experience, no matter how small, strongly impacted her story. A few years before her death, she said, "Many people think that my life has been exemplary and worthy of interest. Of course, as I have been living it all along the way, it has its charms to me as well."

Nature

Jones Very

The bubbling brook doth leap when I come by,
Because my feet find measure with its call;
The birds know when the friend they love is nigh,
For I am known to them, both great and small;
The flower that on the lovely hill-side grows
Expects me there when spring its bloom has given;
And many a tree and bush my wanderings knows,
And e'en the clouds and silent stars of heaven;
For he who with his Maker walks aright,
Shall be their lord as Adam was before;
His ear shall catch each sound with new delight,
Each object wear the dress that then it wore;
And he, as when erect in soul he stood,
Hear from his Father's lips that all is good.

Always Another Spring

May Smith White

Come walk with me when spring is new
And the jasmine rings small bells of gold
And the grass wears diamonds washed in dew—
Come, leave behind the winter's cold.

Here we shall watch the bluebirds nest
And the mountain paths turn green again;
And the heart will find its hidden quest
As the world forgets late winter's rain.

Come while the earth throbs new with spring,
And come for joyous remembering.

Blue lupine hugs a mountainside in Washington. Photograph by Dick Dietrich.

Ideals' Family Recipes

Please send us your best-loved recipes! Mail a typed copy of the recipe along with your name, address, and phone number to Ideals, ATTN: Recipes, P.O. Box 305300, Nashville, Tennessee 37230. We will pay $10 for each recipe used. Meanwhile, try these recipes featuring the fresh aroma of citrus, a perfect accompaniment to a brisk spring day.

Lemon Nut Bread
Phyllis M. Peters of Three Rivers, Michigan

2¼ cups all-purpose flour
1 cup granulated sugar
1 teaspoon baking powder
½ teaspoon salt
1 cup chopped walnuts
1 egg, beaten

2 teaspoons grated lemon peel
1 teaspoon lemon juice
¾ cup evaporated milk
½ cup water
¼ cup melted butter

Preheat oven to 375° F. In a medium bowl, sift together flour, sugar, baking powder, and salt. Set aside. In a large bowl combine remaining ingredients. Stir well. Stir in dry ingredients. Pour mixture into a greased, 9-by-5-by-3-inch loaf pan. Bake 40 minutes or until a toothpick inserted in the middle comes out clean. Makes 1 loaf.

Spring Orange Custards
Becky Dison of Mt. Juliet, Tennessee

4 eggs
2 cups milk
½ cup granulated sugar
½ teaspoon orange extract, divided

⅛ teaspoon salt
½ cup whipping cream
2 teaspoons granulated sugar

Preheat oven to 325° F. In a medium bowl, beat eggs slightly. Stir in milk, ½ cup sugar, ¼ teaspoon of the orange extract, and salt. Place 6 ungreased 6-ounce custard cups in a 13-by-9-by-2-inch baking pan. Divide custard mixture evenly among the cups. Set pan on the oven rack. Carefully pour boiling water into the pan around the cups to a depth of 1 inch. Bake 30 to 45 minutes or until a knife inserted at the edge of a cup comes out clean. Remove cups from pan and cool on a wire rack. Cover and chill for one hour.

In a small mixing bowl, combine whipping cream, ¼ teaspoon orange extract, and 2 teaspoons sugar. Beat until soft peaks form. Spoon on top of the custards. Makes 6 servings.

Key Lime Pie
Dessa Boone of Brentwood, Tennessee

3 egg yolks
1 14-ounce can sweetened condensed milk

½ cup key lime juice
1 baked 9-inch pastry shell

Preheat oven to 350° F. In a medium bowl, beat egg yolks. Stir in condensed milk and key lime juice, mixing well. Pour mixture into pastry shell. Bake 12 to 15 minutes or until set. Cool on wire rack. Chill before serving. Makes 6 to 8 servings.

Lemon Tea Cookies
Janice Reineke of Petersburg, Illinois

1¾ cup all-purpose flour
1 teaspoon baking powder
¼ teaspoon baking soda
¼ teaspoon salt
½ cup butter, softened

1½ cups granulated sugar, divided
½ cup milk
1½ teaspoons vinegar
1 egg
¼ cup plus 1 teaspoon lemon juice

Preheat oven to 350° F. In a medium bowl, sift together flour, baking powder, baking soda, and salt. Set aside. In a medium bowl, cream butter with ¾ cup sugar. Set aside. In a small bowl, combine milk and vinegar and add to butter mixture. Add egg and 1 teaspoon lemon juice. Stir well. Stir in dry ingredients. Drop mixture by spoonfuls onto a greased baking sheet. Bake 15 to 20 minutes or until golden. Remove to wire rack. In a small bowl, combine ¾ cup sugar with ¼ cup lemon juice and stir well to form a glaze. While cookies are still warm, brush with glaze. Makes approximately 2 dozen cookies.

Orange Pound Cake
Elaine B. Porter of Arlington, Massachusetts

2 cups all-purpose flour
½ teaspoon baking powder
⅔ cup butter
1¼ cups granulated sugar

⅔ cup milk
1 teaspoon orange extract
3 eggs

Preheat oven to 300° F. In a medium bowl, sift together flour and baking powder; set aside. In a medium bowl, cream butter with sugar until light and fluffy. Add milk and extract; stir well. Stir in dry ingredients and beat until smooth. Add eggs, one at a time, beating well after each addition. Grease and lightly flour a 9-by-5-by-3-inch loaf pan. Spoon mixture into pan. Bake 1 hour and 25 to 30 minutes or until a toothpick inserted in the middle comes out clean. Makes 8 servings.

Sanctuary

Sudie Stuart Hager

My garden is a place of prayer.
I see my blessings clearest there,
For though my house is plain and small,
It changes to a festive hall
When at my door the crocus blooms,
And I can liven drabbest rooms
With daffodils, verbenas, stocks,
Petunias, columbine, and phlox;
Store crimson leaves and straw bouquets
For cheeriness in winter days.

The pain and bitterness I've known
Fade when I pick a rose half-blown;
And when new trials mock ahead,
I kneel beside a pansy bed.

God talked with man in Eden's shade;
Christ sought a garden when He prayed.

A gardener's patience is rewarded with a beautiful spring show
in New Bern, North Carolina. Photograph by William
Johnson/Johnson's Photography.

Who Has Seen the Wind?
Christina Rossetti

Who has seen the wind?
Neither I nor you;
But when the leaves hang trembling
The wind is passing through.

Who has seen the wind?
Neither you nor I;
But when the trees bow down their heads
The wind is passing by.

Let There Be Kites Again
Glenn Ward Dresbach

Let there be kites again—
Up, up, like wings,
And boys running by,
Holding tight to the strings,
With their eyes to the sky . . .
They will soon be men.

Let there be shouting now—
With wind and cloud
Racing over, and swift
Lean shadows, and proud
Young faces that lift
With light on the brow.

Let there be kites again—
Up, up, from the hill
Each spring of the year,
Over lands we till . . .
There was wonder here
And we found it . . . then.

Two young brothers share a day of kite flying at the beach. Photograph by Dianne Dietrich Leis.

BITS & PIECES

You can't catch the wind in a net.
Charles Haddon Spurgeon

The roots grow deep
when the winds are strong.
Charles R. Swindoll

If you once get to nature's God, and believe Him, and love
Him, it is surprising how easy it is to hear music in the waves,
and songs in the wild whisperings of the winds.
Charles Haddon Spurgeon

The wind of God is always blowing,
but you must hoist your sail.
François Fénelon

Wherever the Son of God goes,
the winds of God are blowing.
Helmut Thielicke

We cannot direct the wind, but we can adjust the sails.
Author Unknown

O ye winds of God, bless ye the Lord: praise him, and
magnify him forever.
Prayer Book, 1662

If the roots are deep,
no fear that the wind will uproot the tree.
Chinese Proverb

We must wait for God . . . in the wind.
Frederick William Faber

Springtime Days

Johanna Ter Wee

Springtime days are for weaving dreams
And taking delight in meandering streams,
For welcoming robins and thrilling to see
The swelling buds on each shrub and tree.
Springtime days are for fragrance and song
When frogs sing in chorus a hundred strong,
For bluebells and tulips and numberless things —
Treasures surpassing the riches of kings.

Spring

Esther Moorefield Lea

Spring is many things like these —
Trailing fronds of willow leaves
Dawning in awakening glade,
Music that the wind harp made,
Dewy daisies wild and sweet
Kneeling softly at my feet,
Winnowing of unseen wings.
Spring is many lovely things.

Two friends enjoy the pleasures of a springtime afternoon. Photograph by K & H Benser/Zefa/H. Armstrong Roberts.

Readers' Forum

◄Marsha Reavis of Houston, Texas, a new subscriber to *Ideals*, shares this springtime photo of her grandson Kyle Lee Milam. One-year-old Kyle sits happily among the bluebonnets that cover the ground at the Brazos State Park in Texas.

◄ Young cousins Anna-Martin Fritts and Travis Fritts show off their spring finery in this snapshot sent to us by their grandmother, Imogene Fritts of Thomasville, North Carolina. Imogene says that Anna-Martin and Travis, who live one hundred miles away, love to see a new calf or feed carrots to the neighbor's ponies during their visits.

Thank you Marsha Reavis, Imogene Fritts, Brenda and Cecil Triplett, and Sandi and Mike Himes for sharing your family photographs with *Ideals*. We hope to hear from other readers who would like to share snapshots with the *Ideals* family. Please include a self-addressed, stamped envelope if you would like the photos returned. Keep your original photographs for safekeeping and send duplicate photos along with your name, address, and telephone number to:

Readers' Forum
Ideals Publications Inc.
P.O. Box 305300
Nashville, Tennessee 37230

ideals®

Publisher, Patricia A. Pingry
Editor, Michelle Prater Burke
Designer, Eve DeGrie
Copy Editor, Kristi Richardson
Editorial Assistant, Christine Landry
Contributing Editors, Lansing Christman, Deana Deck, Pamela Kennedy, Patrick McRae, Nancy Skarmeas

▲   What better way to enjoy the beautiful weather than on a blanket in your grandparents' backyard? Three-year-old Mackenzie Triplett and three-month-old Peyton Clark are doing just that in this picture sent to us by proud grandparents Brenda and Cecil Triplett of Lenoir, North Carolina. Brenda tells us that the children already enjoy looking at all the pictures in *Ideals!*

ACKNOWLEDGMENTS

DOUGLAS, MARJORY STONEMAN. From the book *The Everglades: River of Grass* 50th Anniversary Edition, copyright © 1997 by Marjory Stoneman Douglas. Used by permission of Pineapple Press, Inc. GUEST, EDGAR A. "Creation" from *The Friendly Way*. Reprinted with the permission of Henry Sobell, Jr. JAQUES, EDNA. "Earth's Fragrance" from *Hills of Home*. Copyright © in Canada by Thomas Allen & Son Limited. Reprinted by permission of the publisher. MURTON, JESSIE WILMORE. "Mountains" from *The Shining Thread*. Reprinted by permission of Pacific Press Publishing Association, Inc. STOREY, VIOLET ALLEYN. "For Water" from *A Poet Prays*. Reprinted by permission of Christian Science Monitor.

◄   Sandi and Mike Himes of Greenville, Texas, have a special place in their hearts for their granddaughter Chandler. In this picture, three-year-old Chandler, who is visually impaired, is discovering the special softness and fragrance of a flower from her grandparents' garden. Sandi and Mike tell us that Chandler has a sweet spirit and a memory for details that constantly amazes them!

The Joys of Easter

Edith Helstern

Let Easter joys be in your heart,
Let skies above be blue,
Then may your dearest hopes and dreams
Come swiftly, sweetly true.
And as the Easter days go by,
Let all their cheer remain
To echo always in your heart
In loving, glad refrain.

UNITED STATES POSTAL SERVICE • REQUIRED BY 39 U.S.C. 3685 • STATEMENT OF OWNERSHIP, MANAGEMENT, AND CIRCULATION

1. Publication Title: Ideals. 2. Publication No.: 0019-137X. 3. Filing Date: 9/29/98. 4. Issue Frequency: 6 times a year, January, March, May, July, September, and November. 5. No. of Issues Published Annually: Six. 6. Annual Subscription Price: $19.95. 7. Complete Mailing Address of Known Office of Publication: 535 Metroplex Dr., Ste. 250, PO Box 305300, Davidson County, Nashville, TN 37230-5300. 8. Complete Mailing Address of Headquarters or General Business Office of Publisher: 535 Metroplex Dr., Ste. 250, PO Box 305300, Davidson County, Nashville, TN 37230-5300. 9. Full Names and Complete Mailing Addresses of Publisher, Editor, and Managing Editor: Publisher: Patricia A. Pingry, 535 Metroplex Dr., Ste. 250, Nashville, TN 37211; Editor: Michelle Burke, 535 Metroplex Dr., Ste. 250, Nashville, TN 37211; Managing Editor: Michelle Burke, 535 Metroplex Dr., Ste. 250, Nashville, TN 37211. 10. Owner (Full Name and Complete Mailing Address): Ideals Publications Incorporated, 535 Metroplex Dr., Ste. 250, Nashville, TN 37211. Stockholders Owning or Holding 1 Percent or More of Total Amount of Stock: Simon Waterlow, President, 535 Metroplex Dr., Ste. 250, Nashville, TN 37211; Martin Flanagan, Vice President, Finance, 535 Metroplex Dr., Ste. 250, Nashville, TN 37211. 11. Known Bondholders, Mortgagees, and Other Security Holders Owning or Holding 1 Percent or More of Total Amount of Bonds, Mortgages, or Other Securities: Egmont Foundation, Vognmagergade II, 1148 Copenhagen K, Denmark and Star Bank, 814 Church Street, Nashville, TN 37203. 12. For completion by nonprofit organizations authorized to mail at special rates: Not Applicable. 13. Publication Title: Ideals. 14. Issue Date for Circulation Data Below: Friendship, July 1998. 15. Extent and Nature of Circulation: Average No. Copies Each Issue During Preceding 12 Months: A. Total No. Copies (Net Press Run): 209,649. B. Paid and/or Requested Circulation: (1) Sales Through Dealers and Carriers, Street Vendors, and Counter Sales: 26,256. (2) Paid or Requested Mail Subscriptions: 163,781. C. Total Paid and/or Requested Circulation: 190,037. D. Free Distribution by Mail: 0. E. Free Distribution Outside the Mail: 0. F. Total Free Distribution: 0. G. Total Distribution: 190,037. H. Copies Not Distributed: (1) Office Use, Leftovers, Spoiled: 10,802. (2) Returns from News Agents: 8,812. I. Total: 209,649. Percent Paid and/or Requestion Circulation: 100%. Actual No. Copies of Single Issue Published Nearest to Filing Date: A. Total No. Copies (Net Press Run): 164,729. Paid and/or Requested Circulation: (1) Sales Through Dealers and Carriers, Street Vendors, and Counter Sales: 9,260. (2) Paid or Requested Mail Subscriptions: 153,548. C. Total Paid and/or Requested Circulation: 162,808. D. Free Distribution by Mail: 0. E. Free Distribution Outside the Mail: 0. F. Total Free Distribution: 0. G. Total Distribution: 162,808. H. Copies Not Distributed: (1) Office Use, Leftovers, Spoiled: 1,638. (2) Returns from News Agents: 283. I. Total: 164,729. Percent Paid and/or Requested Circulation: 100%. I certify that all information furnished is true and complete. Rose A. Yates, Vice President, Systems and Operations